INSIDE MEN'S COLLEGE BASKETBALL™

BASKETBALL IN THE BIG TEN CONFERENCE

rosen publishing's
rosen central

GABRIEL KAUFMAN

New York

To my Big Ten basketball friends from Illinois

Published in 2008 by The Rosen Publishing Group, Inc.
29 East 21st Street, New York, NY 10010

First Edition

Library of Congress Cataloging-in-Publication Data

Kaufman, Gabriel.
Inside men's college basketball : basketball in the Big Ten Conference / Gabriel Kaufman. — 1st ed.
    p. cm. — (Inside men's college basketball)
Includes bibliographical references and index.
ISBN-13: 978-1-4042-1383-8 (library binding)
1. Big Ten Conference (U.S.)—Juvenile literature. 2. Basketball—United States—Middle West—Juvenile literature. I. Title.
GV885.415.B547K38 2008
796.323'630973—dc22

                                                                2007029519

Manufactured in the United States of America

On the cover: *(Top)* University of Illinois players Shaun Pruitt, Charles Jackson, and Dee Brown during a pre-game huddle on January 28, 2006. *(Bottom)* Ohio State Buckeye Mike Conley Jr. (1) shoots over Wisconsin Badger Greg Stiemsma's (34) block during the Big Ten tournament final on March 11, 2007.

CONTENTS

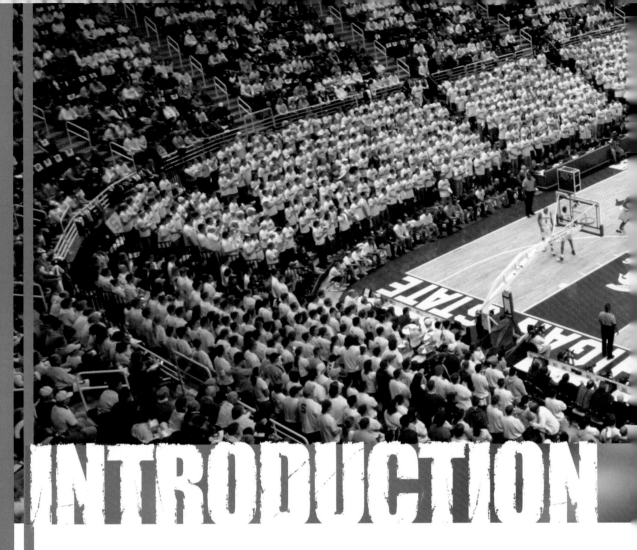

INTRODUCTION

Big Ten basketball fans are passionate about their conference, and for good reason. It's not just because of the exciting games and the talented players, though the conference certainly has both. What really makes the Big Ten special to its fans are the qualities that set it apart from the other conferences. It has a unique history, league rivalries that are renewed every year, colorful coaches, and lively arenas where memories of great seasons live forever. Each season, Big Ten fans have the thrill of watching the next chapter in conference history unfold right before their eyes.

The Big Ten is one of the nation's elite basketball conferences. The league sends many teams to the NCAA tournament each year,

A packed house takes in the Spartan action at Michigan State's Breslin Center. *Inset:* The Big Ten logo, with its "hidden" 11.

and conference schools have advanced all the way to the Final Four on thirty-nine occasions—more than any other conference in the nation. Include the fact that conference teams have won ten NCAA championships, and it's easy to see why the Big Ten has a special place in the college basketball landscape.

Today, the competition is intense both on and off the court. College coaches battle year-round as they try to recruit the best high school players. New players enter the conference, giving fans hope that the current season will be better than the last. Every year brings another round of wins and losses, and the rivalries become even richer. The names and faces of Big Ten basketball are always changing, yet the excitement stays high.

CHAPTER 1

A History of Big Ten Basketball

The Big Ten Conference, formed more than 100 years ago, was created to address many of the same problems that face college sports today. In the late 1800s, the popularity of college sports was increasing rapidly. Football had just been invented and was an immediate hit. Students and fans began following their football teams with intense interest.

Despite the growing popularity, some people were concerned that college sports were heading in the wrong direction. With increased fan attention, teams were suddenly under more pressure to win. As a result, many teams began to cheat to gain an advantage. Professional athletes were being paid to play for college teams. Students who were failing in the classroom were allowed to compete on the field. It was becoming clear that schools were losing control of their sports teams and that college athletics needed regulations.

A Big Idea

Purdue University president James H. Smart was one of the first people to take action. He arranged for a meeting to address these problems. On January 11, 1895, a group of university presidents from neighboring schools met at the Palmer House hotel in Chicago, Illinois. In attendance were the presidents from the University of Chicago, the University of Illinois, the University of Michigan, the University of Minnesota, Northwestern University, Purdue University, and the University of Wisconsin.

Purdue University president James H. Smart, pictured here in 1891, was a key player in the creation of the Big Ten conference.

The seven presidents agreed on several principles that each school's teams would follow. First, only full-time students would be allowed to participate. Second, students could not be paid to play. Finally, students would not be allowed to compete if they were earning failing grades in the classroom. These rules not only laid the groundwork for the creation of the Big Ten Conference, but they also came to serve as a model for all modern college athletics.

The seven schools decided to form an organization called the Intercollegiate Conference of Faculty Representatives, or ICFR. It was the first collegiate sports conference in the United States. Teams in the conference would play against each other with the assurance that each member was following a standard set of rules.

Growing Bigger

The new seven-member conference was an immediate success. The rules ensured fair competition, and the league format proved popular with fans. Other schools became eager to join. In 1899, Indiana University and the University of Iowa were added to the ICFR (also known as the Western Conference), which then became known as the Big Nine. Ohio State was the next school to join, in 1912. When Michigan rejoined the conference in 1917, after a ten-year departure, the conference had ten schools. The league became known as the Big Ten, a name that would stick through the years, even though the conference would not always have ten members.

In 1946, the University of Chicago became the first school to permanently leave the conference. Michigan State University replaced Chicago in 1949, and when Penn State University joined

Loud and Proud

Part of the excitement of Big Ten basketball is the large, loud crowds that pack its stands. In 2006–2007, the conference led the nation in attendance for the thirty-first straight season as 2,470,250 fans crammed into Big Ten arenas.

Student-cheering sections at Big Ten basketball games are especially rowdy and skilled at irritating players on opposing teams. Every student section in the conference has its own name, which usually references the team's colors, coach, or mascot. All real Big Ten fans know, for instance, that their team will have to deal with the Orange Crush section when they travel to Illinois. The Izzone at Michigan State, named after Spartan coach Tom Izzo, is always a formidable presence at Spartan games, and the Crimson Crew will certainly try its best to create a hostile environment for teams playing at Indiana.

the conference in 1990, the league had eleven members. The conference decided to keep "Ten" in its name, however, for the sake of tradition and name recognition. The fact that there are actually eleven league members is represented in the "hidden" number 11 in the official conference logo.

Starting Small

Today, college basketball is one of the most popular sports in America. It is therefore hard to imagine that few people even noticed when the first college basketball game took place more than 100 years ago.

In 1891, Dr. James Naismith invented the game of basketball at

Dr. James Naismith (1861–1939) invented basketball in 1891. The first game was played with a soccer ball and two peach baskets for goals.

a YMCA (Young Men's Christian Association) training school in Springfield, Massachusetts. One person who embraced the new sport was Naismith's friend and coworker Amos Alonzo Stagg, a football coach. When Stagg accepted a job at the University of Chicago, he brought the game of basketball with him to the Midwest. Stagg helped organize the Chicago Maroons' first basketball team and promoted the idea of playing with five players on each side, a number that is standard today (it was common at the time for teams to play seven to nine players on a side). On January 18, 1896, the first

CURRENT BIG TEN TEAMS AND THEIR ACCOMPLISHMENTS

SCHOOL	TEAM NAME	YEAR JOINED BIG TEN	BIG TEN REGULAR SEASON CONFERENCE CHAMPIONSHIPS	BIG TEN TOURNAMENT TITLES	NCAA TOURNAMENT APPEARANCES
University of Illinois	Fighting Illini	1896	17	2	27
Indiana University	Hoosiers	1899	20	0	34
University of Iowa	Hawkeyes	1899	8	2	22
University of Michigan	Wolverines	1896	12	0	16
Michigan State University	Spartans	1949	10	2	21
University of Minnesota	Golden Gophers	1896	8	0	6
Northwestern University	Wildcats	1896	2	0	0
Ohio State University	Buckeyes	1912	17	2	20
Penn State University	Nittany Lions	1990	0	0	8
Purdue University	Boilermakers	1896	21	0	21
University of Wisconsin	Badgers	1896	16	1	13

college basketball game with five players on each side took place. Coach Stagg's Chicago team beat Iowa 13–12 at the Iowa Armory in front of 400 fans, and modern basketball was under way. The Big Ten's first official basketball season took place ten years later, in 1906.

Big Programs

The Big Ten has always been one of the strongest basketball conferences in the nation. Many of its schools have strong basketball programs, which is one of the reasons conference play is so competitive every year. Big Ten teams have made thirty-nine NCAA Final

NCAA TOURNAMENT WINS/LOSSES (winning percentage)	NCAA FINAL FOUR APPEARANCES	NCAA CHAMPIONSHIPS	BIG TEN CONFERENCE PLAYERS OF THE YEAR	FIRST-ROUND NBA DRAFT PICKS
38–28 (.576)	5	0	4	14
60–29 (.674)	8	5	15	21
27–24 (.529)	3	0	3	8
34–15 (.694)	4	1	6	20
41–20 (.672)	6	2	6	16
7–6 (.538)	0	0	4	18
0–0 (.000)	0	0	0	0
37–19 (.661)	9	1	5	19
9–10 (.474)	1	0	0	0
28–21 (.571)	2	0	2	6
17–12 (.586)	2	1	5	7

Four appearances—more than any other conference in the country. They have won ten NCAA championships, second behind the Pac-10 Conference. Since the 2000 season, the Big Ten is the only conference to advance five different teams to the Final Four.

The two teams from the state of Indiana—the Purdue Boilermakers and the Indiana University Hoosiers—have had the most success in conference play. Purdue ranks first in league history with twenty-one total Big Ten championships. Indiana places second with twenty. While the Boilermakers hold a slight edge in conference titles, the Hoosiers have had far more success in postseason play. They have reached the Final Four on eight occasions, winning five NCAA

Ohio State's Greg Oden (20) shoots over Florida's Al Horford in the 2007 NCAA championship game.

championships. Purdue, on the other hand, has had a hard time turning regular season triumph into postseason success. They have made only two Final Four appearances and have yet to win an NCAA championship.

Illinois, Michigan State, and Ohio State all boast strong programs that have consistently made the NCAA tournament. The Fighting Illini have made the NCAA tournament twenty-seven times, the second most in the conference to Indiana's thirty-four. The Ohio State Buckeyes have reached the Final Four nine times, more than any other conference team. Illinois and Ohio State are tied for third in conference titles with seventeen.

Michigan State has experienced tremendous NCAA tournament success in recent years. The Spartans have earned trips to four of the last nine Final Fours, including three in a row from 1999 to 2001. They have won two NCAA titles, in 1979 and 2000. In 2007, ESPN.com ranked Michigan State as the second best program in the country over the last ten years.

The Big Ten's Greatest Coaches

Big names, big personalities, and big achievements dominate the list of the Big Ten's best coaches. While players come and go in college basketball, coaches often remain the one constant for each team. Fans become familiar not only with each coach's offensive and defensive strategies, but also with his sideline habits, career accomplishments, and off-the-court personality.

Early Innovators

The Big Ten has been home to many great coaches through the years. Two early standouts were Purdue's Ward "Piggy" Lambert and Wisconsin's Walter "Doc" Meanwell. Lambert and Meanwell were important coaches not just because of their winning records and conference titles. They were also innovators who changed the way the sport was played.

Coach Lambert gives instruction to his players, c. 1930. Future basketball Hall of Famer John Wooden is kneeling on the right.

Meanwell coached the Wisconsin Badgers from 1912 to 1917 and again from 1921 to 1934. He led the team to a record of 246–99 (.712 winning percentage) and won nine Big Ten championships. One of the country's most influential coaches at the time, Meanwell moved away from the rough, physical play that was common. He instead developed a style of offense that emphasized crisp passing and set plays.

Piggy Lambert coached the Boilermakers during the 1917 season and from 1919 to 1945. He earned a career record of 371–152 (.709 winning percentage), while capturing eleven conference titles. Lambert left his mark on the game by introducing the fast break, a play in which teams move the ball quickly up the court in an effort to score before the opposing team has a chance to set up its defense.

The General

The league has never seen a coach more loved by his fans and disliked by his critics than Bob Knight, who coached Indiana University from 1971 to 2000. No matter how people feel about Knight, "the General" was arguably the best coach the conference has ever seen. A quick look at his career numbers supports his case. Knight has the most conference wins of any coach in league history (353) and the highest conference winning percentage (.700). He is tied with Piggy Lambert for the most Big Ten titles (11). He also won Big Ten Coach of the Year honors on six occasions.

Former Indiana coach Bob Knight, above, reacts to an official's call during a 1994 game. Knight's record of 353 conference victories is the most in Big Ten history.

Knight's teams won four consecutive conference titles from 1973 to 1976. In addition, the 1976 team was the last in NCAA history to remain undefeated throughout an entire season and go on to win the NCAA championship. Indiana enjoyed great NCAA tournament success during the Knight era, making five Final Fours and winning three NCAA championships (1976, 1983, and 1987). Overall, Knight's teams made twenty-four NCAA appearances, recording an impressive 42–21 record in tourney play.

Despite his excellent record on the court, it was often Knight's behavior and not his coaching ability that received the most attention. Knight was famous for his quick temper. He was frequently combative with referees, members of the press, and even his own players. Several former Indiana players accused Knight of both verbal and physical abuse. As a result of repeated problems concerning his behavior, Indiana fired Knight on September 10, 2000. Many people therefore believe his career has been severely tarnished.

Controversy aside, there is little doubt that Knight is one of the greatest coaches in college basketball history. He thus far holds a career record of 832–322, which places him third on the NCAA all-time wins list. He is currently head coach at Texas Tech University and has a great chance of setting a new all-time wins record.

Will the Wildcats Ever Win?

Northwestern has always been one of the weakest programs in the Big Ten. Since 1906, the Wildcats have won only two conference titles and have never earned a trip to the NCAA tournament. Since the 2001–2002 season, when he took over the program, coach Bill Carmody has been trying to reverse the Wildcats' losing tradition.

Carmody brought with him a reputation for being an offensive mastermind. In his first seven years at Northwestern, however, the Wildcats experienced mixed results. Their high point came in 2004 when they finished conference play with an 8–8 record, the school's best record since the 1968 season. This improvement earned Carmody Big Ten Coach of the Year honors. There's little doubt that Carmody has made Northwestern more competitive overall. Nonetheless, they have yet to finish over .500 in conference play and are still searching for their first NCAA tournament bid. Only time will tell if Carmody can get Northwestern over the hump.

"Mean Gene" Keady

Longtime Purdue coach Gene Keady is one of the most successful, if not recognizable, coaching figures in Big Ten history. Known for his fiery personality and the permanent scowl he wore on the sidelines, Keady finished his career with the second most wins in conference history (262) and the third-best winning percentage (.661).

During Keady's coaching reign, from 1981 to 2005, the Boilermakers captured six Big Ten titles, including three straight from 1994 to 1996. While Keady never enjoyed the post-season success that in-state rival Bob Knight did at Indiana, his teams were no strangers to tournament play. They earned seventeen trips to

During his last season as the Boilermakers' head coach, Gene Keady reacts to action on the court during a 2004–2005 game.

the NCAA tournament. Keady was named National Coach of the Year six times and Big Ten Coach of the Year seven times, the most in league history. Keady will be remembered for his intense, entertaining coaching style and his ability to get the most out of his players.

Today's Coaches

Michigan State's Tom Izzo is one of the country's most accomplished current coaches. He has built a powerhouse program that produces

Players watch from the bench during a game as Wisconsin coach Bill Ryan talks to his assistant coach. (*From left to right*): assistant coach Greg Gard, Joe Krabbenhoft, Brian Butch, Marcus Landry, Ray Nixon, Greg Stiemsma, Coach Ryan, Tanner Bronson, Kevin Gullikson, Morris Cain, and Devin Barry.

top teams year in and year out. Since taking over the Spartans' program in 1996, Izzo has led Michigan State to four Big Ten titles, four Final Four appearances, and one NCAA championship in 2000. He has received four National Coach of the Year awards and is on track to become one of the conference's all-time great coaches.

Current Illinois head coach Bruce Weber took over the Illini's program in 2004 and has been winning games at a record-breaking pace ever since. Thus far, he has 112 victories, the most wins ever by a Big Ten coach in his first four years. In addition, he is the only coach to win two outright Big Ten titles in his first two years. In 2004–2005, Weber coached Illinois to a record of 37–2, its best season in school history. The thirty-seven wins tied the all-time NCAA record for most wins in one season. The Illini also made it to the 2005 NCAA championship game, although they lost to North Carolina by a score of 75–70.

Wisconsin has emerged as one of the top programs in the league since Bo Ryan took over the Badgers prior to the 2001–2002 season. Ryan has guided Wisconsin to the four winningest seasons in Badger history, including a thirty-win season in 2006–2007, which set the school record for wins. Wisconsin has won two conference titles under Ryan's leadership and seems poised to remain a conference power for years to come.

Ohio State coach Thad Matta has enjoyed tremendous early success in the Big Ten. Since 2005, Matta has recruited the country's best high school players, turning the Buckeyes into a national power. In his first three seasons, Matta coached the Buckeyes to two outright conference titles. In 2007, he led a young Buckeye club all the way to the NCAA championship game.

The Big Ten's Greatest Players

Whether it's Earvin "Magic" Johnson leading Michigan State to the NCAA championship in 1979 or Glenn "Big Dog" Robinson scoring forty-nine points to clinch the 1994 conference title, every fan has a favorite memory of the Big Ten's brightest stars.

Big Name Buckeyes

The Ohio State Buckeyes' teams of the early 1960s dominated the conference behind the play of Jerry Lucas, John Havlicek, and Larry Siegfried. From 1960 to 1962, the Buckeyes achieved a remarkable record of 78–6, including three conference titles, three trips to the NCAA Final Four, and the 1960 NCAA championship. Lucas was was named Big Ten Player of the Year all three years he played for the Buckeyes. He went on to play in the NBA

(National Basketball Association) and was named one of the fifty Greatest Players in NBA history.

Magic

Earvin "Magic" Johnson is one of the most famous players in NBA history, but his basketball career took shape in 1977, at Michigan State. Johnson arrived on campus having already earned the nickname "Magic" in high school. Standing six feet, nine inches tall, he was big enough to play either the forward or center positions, yet he had the running, dribbling, and passing skills of a point guard.

Magic mostly played point guard in his two seasons at Michigan State. In 1979, he and high-scoring teammate Greg "Special K" Kelser led the

Michigan State legend Earvin "Magic" Johnson charges to the hoop during the 1979 NCAA championship game.

Spartans to their first NCAA championship in school history. With his extraordinary court vision and highlight-reel passes, there certainly seemed to be a little magic in his game.

Hoosier Heroes

A number of players blossomed under Indiana coach Bob Knight in the 1970s and 1980s, helping to propel the Hoosiers to three national championships. In 1976, National Player of the Year Scott May

Flashbulbs illuminate Indiana's Isiah Thomas as he cuts down the net after leading the Hoosiers to the 1981 NCAA championship.

averaged more than twenty-three points per game. He and fellow All-American Kent Benson together led the Hoosiers to a perfect 32–0 record and an NCAA championship. May took home Big Ten Player of the Year honors in 1975 and 1976, while Benson won the award in 1977.

The Hoosiers' 1981 NCAA championship team featured one of the most talented players ever to wear an Indiana uniform. Guard Isiah Thomas's career at Indiana lasted only two years, but in that time, he won two Big Ten titles and an NCAA championship. He led the 1981 team in scoring and was honored as the Most Outstanding Player of the NCAA tournament. Thomas entered the NBA draft after his sophomore season and enjoyed an All-Star NBA career with the Detroit Pistons.

Indiana guard Steve Alford used his long-range shooting skills to help the Hoosiers capture the 1987 NCAA championship. The three-point shot was first introduced to college basketball in the 1986–1987 season, and Alford took advantage of the new rule. He shot a remarkable 53 percent from beyond the three-point arc while averaging twenty-two points per game. This feat earned him Big Ten

Player of the Year honors. After a brief NBA career, Alford returned to the college ranks, this time as a coach. From 2000–2007, he coached his one-time rival, the Iowa Hawkeyes.

Michigan's Fab Five

No discussion of the best players in conference history would be complete without mentioning the Wolverines' "Fab Five." In the autumn of 1991, five highly touted freshmen arrived at Michigan. Chris Webber, Jalen Rose, Juwan Howard, Jimmy King, and Ray Jackson were all top recruits, but few experts thought the players could step in and immediately turn Michigan into a championship contender. The Fab Five proved the experts wrong.

The Fab Five played with an incredible swagger, throwing daring alley-oop passes and slamming home incredible dunks. They led the

The Wizard of Westwood

Most basketball fans are familiar with the name John Wooden. As the coach of the UCLA (University of California, Los Angeles) Bruins from 1949 to 1975, he led his teams to ten NCAA championships, sixteen Final Four appearances, and a remarkable eighty-eight consecutive victories (from 1971 to 1973). He earned the nickname "the Wizard of Westwood" (Westwood is the section of Los Angeles where UCLA is located) for his seemingly magical ability to produce winning teams. For his efforts as a coach, Wooden was elected to the Naismith Hall of Fame in 1972.

What many fans don't realize, however, is that Wooden had already been elected to the Hall of Fame in 1960 as an All-American player. From 1930 to 1932, Wooden led the Purdue Boilermakers to two Big Ten championships. He also set a conference record for most points scored in a season (although his 12.2 scoring average per game would be considered modest by modern standards). Since 1976, the John R. Wooden Award has been presented each year to the top collegiate basketball player in the country.

Chris Webber, seen here slamming down a dunk in the 1992 NCAA tournament, was the headliner of the Fab Five. *Inset:* Coach Steve Fisher *(center)* poses with the four other members of the Fab Five. Clockwise from bottom left are Jimmy King, Jalen Rose, Juwan Howard, and Ray Jackson.

Wolverines all the way to the NCAA championship game in both 1992 and 1993. Unfortunately, however, one cannot find the Fab Five's achievements in the record books. In the late 1990s, the Michigan program was surrounded by scandal as allegations arose that players were receiving illegal payments from university boosters. Chris Webber was one of the players who accepted money. In 2002, Michigan decided to penalize its basketball program for mis- conduct. Michigan erased the 1992 Final Four from record and forfeited the entire 1993 season. Though the Fab Five cannot be found in the record books today, fans who saw them play will never forget their fearless brand of basketball.

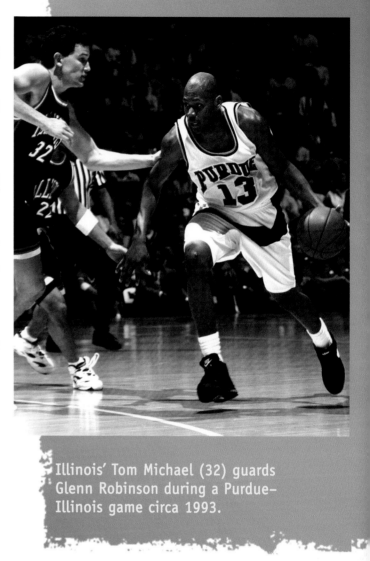

Illinois' Tom Michael (32) guards Glenn Robinson during a Purdue– Illinois game circa 1993.

Cheaney and Robinson

Indiana's Calbert Cheaney and Purdue's Glenn Robinson were both prolific scorers in the 1990s. Cheaney finished his record-breaking career as the conference's all-time leading scorer with 2,614 points. He also led the Hoosiers to the 1993 NCAA Final Four and was the recipient of the Wooden Award that same year.

Robinson, whose nickname was "Big Dog," played only two seasons for the Boilermakers. Still, he left his mark. In the 1993–1994 season, Robinson averaged more than thirty points and ten rebounds per game, leading the Boilermakers to a Big Ten title. His impressive season earned him National Player of the Year honors. Robinson was selected as the first pick in the 1994 NBA draft by the Milwaukee Bucks. He was named an NBA All-Star on two occasions during his professional career.

Big Ten Award Winners

The following is a list of Big Ten athletes who have won national awards. Many other awards are given away each year, but the following are some of the most prestigious.

Naismith Men's College Player of the Year Award (awarded since 1969)
Scott May, Indiana, 1976
Calbert Cheaney, Indiana, 1993
Glenn Robinson, Purdue, 1994

John R. Wooden Player of the Year (awarded since 1976)
Calbert Cheaney, Indiana, 1993
Glenn Robinson, Purdue, 1994

Associated Press Player of the Year (awarded since 1961)
Jerry Lucas, Ohio State, 1961
Jerry Lucas, Ohio State, 1962
Gary Bradds, Ohio State, 1964
Cazzie Russell, Michigan, 1966
Scott May, Indiana, 1976

Calbert Cheaney, Indiana, 1993
Glenn Robinson, Purdue, 1994

NCAA Basketball Tournament Most Outstanding Player (awarded since 1939)
Jimmy Hull, Ohio State, 1939
Marvin Huffman, Indiana, 1940
John Kotz, Wisconsin, 1941
Jerry Lucas, Ohio State, 1960
Jerry Lucas, Ohio State, 1961
Kent Benson, Indiana, 1976
Earvin Johnson, Michigan State, 1979
Isiah Thomas, Indiana, 1981
Keith Smart, Indiana, 1987
Glen Rice, Michigan, 1989
Mateen Cleaves, Michigan State, 2000

New Stars in the New Millennium

Big Ten fans witnessed a changing of the guard in the late 1990s. Powerhouses Indiana, Michigan, and Purdue fell to the middle of the conference pack, while Michigan State and Illinois emerged as the top two programs in the league.

Michigan State captured four consecutive Big Ten championships from 1998 to 2001. They were led by the stellar play of star point guard Mateen Cleaves, All-American forward Morris Peterson, and all-conference guard Charlie Bell. No player was more responsible for the Spartans' rise to prominence than Cleaves, a two-time conference player of the year who finished his career as the Big Ten's all-time career assists leader. Cleaves was named Most Outstanding Player of the 2000 NCAA tournament after he led the Spartans to their second NCAA championship in school history.

The 2003–2004 and 2004–2005 seasons saw Illinois dominate the conference behind the sensational play of its athletic three-guard lineup. Led by super-quick Dee Brown, the Illini won back-to-back outright conference championships for the first time since 1951 and 1952. Brown joined with first-team all–Big Ten guard Luther Head and future NBA star Deron Williams to lead Illinois to the 2005 NCAA championship game for the first time in school history.

While Head and Williams were both all-conference performers who went on to become first-round NBA picks, it was Brown who stood out as the leader of the Illini. The flashy point guard was often the smallest player on the court, but his size didn't prevent him from becoming one of the most accomplished college athletes in the country. Among the honors he received were the 2005 Big Ten Player of the Year and Big Ten Defensive Player of the Year awards, and the 2006 Bob Cousy Award, which recognizes the nation's top point guard.

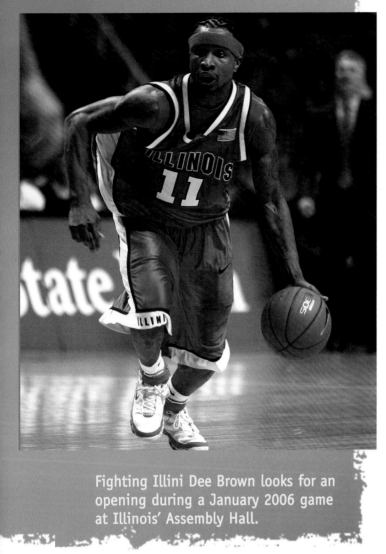

Fighting Illini Dee Brown looks for an opening during a January 2006 game at Illinois' Assembly Hall.

The 2007 Big Ten season had plenty of star power, starting with Ohio State's seven-foot freshman phenom Greg Oden. Entering the league as one of the most hyped freshmen in college basketball history, Oden did not disappoint. He led the Buckeyes to a Big Ten championship and a trip to the NCAA championship game. He earned first-team all–Big Ten honors and became the first freshman in conference history to win the Defensive Player of the Year Award. Oden left Ohio State after just one season and was selected by the Portland Trail Blazers with the number-one pick in the NBA draft.

While Oden received much of the attention on the national stage, it was Wisconsin forward Alando Tucker who proved to be the best player in the conference in 2006–2007. Tucker averaged twenty points per game and led Wisconsin to their highest single-season win total in school history (30–6). He won Big Ten Player of the Year honors and ended his college career with 2,217 points, setting the record as the Badgers' all-time leading scorer. Tucker was selected in the first round of the 2007 NBA draft by the Phoenix Suns.

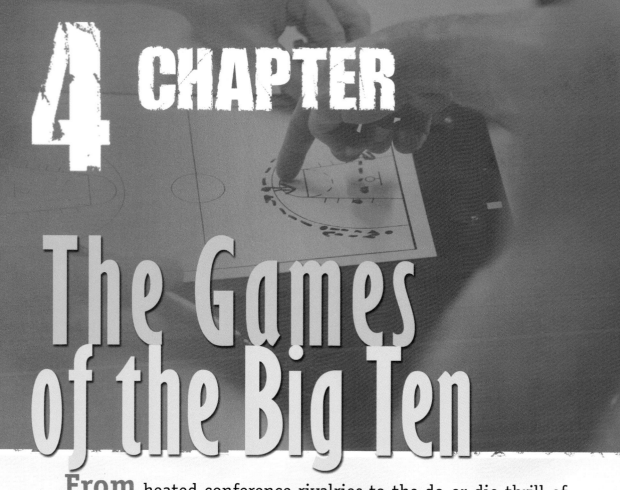

4 CHAPTER

The Games of the Big Ten

From heated conference rivalries to the do-or-die thrill of the NCAA tournament, it's the intensity of Big Ten games that make them so exciting to watch. The anticipation of a big game can capture fans' imaginations for weeks before the actual game is played. Likewise, the thrill of victory, or disappointment of defeat, can linger for days after the final buzzer has sounded. Each year brings memorable games that make the league's rivalries and history even richer and more exciting.

Rivalries

Conference teams play each other at least once during the sixteen-game conference schedule, and most teams play each other twice. With so much at stake, it's not surprising that most fans consider every league opponent a rival.

Illinois and Indiana have competed against each other for more than 100 years. Above, Illinois' Calvin Brock (25) shoots over two Indiana defenders during the 2007 Big Ten tournament.

Illinois and Indiana

Illinois has the most all-time conference wins in league history with 845. Indiana has the second most with 827. Each school has played in the Big Ten since 1905, and for more than 100 years both schools have consistently fielded talented basketball teams. The teams are so evenly matched, in fact, that since 1905 they have played each other practically to a draw (Indiana holds a slight series lead, 80–78). With the two schools' close proximity

Above, a battle between Indiana and Purdue begins with the opening tip-off of a January 2005 game at the Boilermakers' Mackey Arena.

and proud basketball traditions, it's only natural that Illinois and Indiana have developed one of the best rivalries in the conference.

Purdue and Indiana University

Both schools are located in the basketball-crazy state of Indiana. And consider the fact that Purdue and Indiana have the two most successful programs in league history, and you have one of the fiercest rivalries in college basketball. The competition is so intense that even the coaches can get carried away. In one of the most famous incidents of his career, Bob Knight was so enraged by a referee's call during a 1985 Hoosier–Boilermaker game that he threw a chair across the court.

Fans love to debate which team has the better basketball program. While Purdue has the better head-to-head record (107–83) and more all-time Big Ten titles (21 to Indiana's 20), Indiana has experienced far more success in the NCAA tournament. The Hoosiers have won five NCAA championships to the Boilermakers' zero. Each year, another chapter is written, and the debate continues among the fans.

Michigan and Michigan State

Michigan and Michigan State fans pay attention to the annual renewal of this in-state conference rivalry. Although the Wolverines hold the lead in the series with a 91–70 record, it's the Spartans that have recently dominated the series. As of the end of the 2006–2007 season, Michigan State had won fourteen of its last seventeen games against Michigan. With such one-sided domination, the basketball rivalry between the two schools has currently lost a little bit of its edge. It's still one of the most important games on the schedule for each team, however, and always will be no matter what each team's record is entering their matchup.

NCAA Tournament

The NCAA tournament, also known as March Madness or the Big Dance, takes place every March following the completion of the regular season. The sixty-five best teams in the nation are invited to participate, and a school's success or failure in the tournament often defines its season.

Big Ten teams have enjoyed plenty of victories in the tournament, making the Final Four thirty-nine times and winning the championship title on ten occasions. Since Indiana became the first conference team to win the NCAA championship in 1940, Big Ten teams have been a part of some of the most memorable championship games in tournament history.

All–Big Ten Championship

The year 1976 was special for Big Ten basketball. For the first time in NCAA history, two rival teams from the same conference squared off in the championship game. Coach Bob Knight's Hoosiers brought a 31–0 record into the game and were looking to complete a perfect season. The Michigan Wolverines finished second to the Hoosiers in conference play and were looking to win the ultimate prize as consolation.

"The Flintstones"

The most recent Big Ten team to win the NCAA championship was the 2000 Michigan State squad, coached by Tom Izzo. Three players, collectively known as "the Flintstones," starred for the Spartans. Mateen Cleaves, Morris Peterson, and Charlie Bell all grew up together in Flint, Michigan, before attending Michigan State. Cleaves, the point guard, was the heart and soul of the team. It was his inspiring tournament play that gave Michigan State its second NCAA championship in school history.

After grinding out a hard-fought 53–41 semifinal victory over conference rival Wisconsin, the Spartans took on the athletic Florida Gators in the championship game. Michigan State was leading 50–44 with 16:18 left in the second half when Cleaves fell to the floor with a sprained ankle. Nervous Spartan fans across the country watched as their star player was helped off the court. Four minutes later, however, Cleaves was inserted back into the lineup, and he limped onto the court. The Spartans pulled out the victory. For his terrific play and leadership, Cleaves was named the tournament's Most Outstanding Player.

Larry Bird and Magic Johnson first faced each other in the 1979 NCAA final. As Bird (33) guards, Johnson looks to pass to a teammate.

Although the Wolverines entered the game as the heavy underdog, they raced out to a 35–29 advantage behind the play of their star guard, Rickey Green. The talented Hoosiers proved to be too much, however, and went on to win the championship, 86–68. Scott May earned tournament MVP (Most Valuable Player) honors, and Indiana got their perfect 32–0 record. No NCAA champion has ended the season undefeated since.

Magic vs. Bird

When Michigan State played Indiana State for the NCAA championship in 1979, few observers realized they were witnessing the first chapter in what would become one of the great rivalries in basketball's history. The two stars of the game, Michigan State's Magic Johnson and Indiana State's Larry Bird, would continue their rivalry as superstars in the NBA (Johnson's Los Angeles Lakers and Bird's Boston Celtics battled in the NBA finals three times during the 1980s). Before they entered the professional ranks, however, they faced off in one of the most famous championship games in NCAA history. Bird's accurate shooting had carried Indiana State into the title game with a perfect 33–0 record. Magic and the Spartans were too strong for the Sycamores, however, as Michigan State rolled to a 75–64 victory. Many experts believe the highly anticipated game helped turn college basketball into the popular sport that it is today.

The Mascots of the Big Ten

Mascots add to the fun of Big Ten basketball games. Whether they are hanging out on the sidelines, with the band, or in the stands, they always have one goal—to get the crowd excited!

Bucky Badger

Wisconsin's original mascot was a live badger that prowled the sidelines. The wild animal proved difficult to control, however. On several occasions the badger escaped from its handlers and had to be run down before it could hurt anyone. The badger was eventually donated to the Madison Zoo, and a raccoon named Regdab (Badger backward) was brought in as the new mascot. Regdab proved unpopular with fans though, so the search for a new mascot continued.

In 1949, a Wisconsin art student made a papier-mâché badger head, and a fellow student wore the costume to the homecoming football

Bucky Badger cheers on the team with other Wisconsin fans during a 2007 game against Ohio State. The Badgers defeated the Buckeyes, 72–69, on the court of their sold-out Kohl's Center.

game. The campus held a vote to determine a name for the new mascot, and the winner was Buckingham U. Badger, or Bucky for short.

Herky the Hawk

A black bear cub named Burch was Iowa's first mascot. Burch lived under the bleachers at Iowa Field and roamed the sidelines during games. Tragedy struck in 1910, however, when Burch drowned in the Iowa River. A new mascot was needed, and in 1948, a university professor drew a picture of a bird that would become the school's new mascot. The university held a statewide contest to determine the new mascot's name. The winning name was Herky, short for Hercules (a figure in Greek mythology who symbolizes strength). Herky the Hawk made his first appearance at a Hawkeye football game in 1959. He attends both football and basketball games, as well as wrestling matches and swim meets.

Brutus Buckeye

In 1965, members of an Ohio State student organization decided their school needed a mascot. After briefly considering a live buck deer, the group decided that a student should dress as a buckeye, the official tree of the state of Ohio. The name

Ohio State's Brutus Buckeye leads the cheers during the 2007 NCAA tournament.

Brutus resulted from an all-campus naming contest. Brutus Buckeye has been present on the sidelines of Ohio State football and basketball games ever since.

The Nittany Lion

In 1904, the Penn State baseball team traveled to New Jersey to play the Princeton University Tigers. When the Penn State players arrived, Princeton fans taunted them with a statue of a Bengal tiger, saying the fierce cat represented the brutal treatment Penn State was going to receive on the field. At the time, Penn State did not have a mascot

The Nittany Lion, above, appears on court during a break in post-season action during the Big Ten tournament.

of its own, but that did not stop the players from responding to the teasing. One Penn State player replied that an animal called the Nittany Lion lived in the Nittany Mountains surrounding their campus. The lion was so ferocious that it could even defeat a tiger. The Nittany Lion didn't exist, but the name became so popular over the next several years that it became the school's mascot. In 1921, a Penn State student dressed as the Nittany Lion for a game, and the costumed mascot was born.

Sparty

Michigan State's Sparty dresses as a Spartan warrior from ancient Greece.

Chief Illiniwek

For many years, Chief Illiniwek was the official symbol of the University of Illinois. An Illinois student, dressed in Native American clothing, portrayed the chief and performed a dance at halftime during all home basketball and football games.

In the 1970s and 1980s, many people started to criticize Chief Illiniwek. They argued that it was offensive to use an ethnic group as a mascot and that the chief was a Native American stereotype. Supporters of the chief countered that Illiniwek was not a mascot but a symbol intended to honor Native Americans. The critics eventually won. The university decided to retire Chief Illiniwek, who performed his last dance in February 2007.

He is by far the meanest looking mascot in the league. This muscular, cartoonlike character made his first appearance at Michigan State games in 1989 and was an immediate hit with the fans. At games, Sparty likes to hang out and root for the Spartans with the cheerleaders. Fans can also spot Sparty showing off his incredible strength to the crowd by performing one-handed push-ups and flexing his mascot muscles.

Willie the Wildcat

During the 1923 football season, a live bear cub named Furpaw was driven from the local zoo to the Northwestern football field to greet fans as they arrived at the game. Fans loved the cub, but Northwestern

Sparty's muscles have been noticed outside of the Big Ten: he was voted "Buffest Mascot" by *Muscle and Fitness* magazine!

ended the season with a losing record and the team blamed their bad luck on little Furpaw. The team banned the endearing bear from attending all future games.

Northwestern adopted the name "Wildcats" in 1924, after a newspaper columnist compared the football team's ferociousness to that of the animal. It wasn't until 1947, however, that Willie became a mascot. For a homecoming parade float, four fraternity brothers made a Willie the Wildcat costume, and the mascot has existed ever since.

GLOSSARY

allegations Accusations that someone has done something wrong.

alley-oop A high pass near a basketball hoop's rim that is caught by a jumping teammate who dunks the ball.

Big Dance A nickname for the NCAA tournament.

booster A person who promotes an organization or person; in college sports, it often refers to someone who donates money to a university.

combative Eager to argue or fight.

court vision The ability to see the entire court and predict where players will be.

elite The group or groups regarded as being the best.

fast break A play in which the ball is pushed quickly up the court in an effort to score before the other team can set up its defense.

Final Four The last four teams remaining in the NCAA tournament from the original field of sixty-five.

formidable Someone or something that sparks fear or respect from others, often because of size or skill.

headliner The best, or most noteworthy, attraction in a group.

hostile Unfriendly; to act angrily or aggressively toward someone.

innovator A person who changes something by introducing a new method or technique.

March Madness A nickname for the NCAA tournament since the tournament takes place in March.

mastermind A highly intelligent person.

NCAA tournament The annual college basketball tournament sponsored by the National Collegiate Athletic Association; it is single elimination, which means a team is out of the tournament once it loses.

point guard A position on a basketball team that is the primary dribbler and is responsible for running the team's offense.

postseason Tournament games played after the scheduled season is over.

powerhouse An extremely talented team; a team that is significantly better than the majority of its competition.

recruit To attempt to persuade someone to join an organization or a cause.

set play A play designed by the coach in which players perform specific movements and tasks with the goal of scoring a basket.

stereotype A widely held generalization or image of a certain people or thing.

swagger To behave in a confident or arrogant way.

tarnished Having become less valued or respected.

touted Enthusiastically praised or recommended.

FOR MORE INFORMATION

Big Ten Conference
1500 West Higgins Road
Park Ridge, IL 60068-6300
(847) 696-1010
Web site: http://bigten.cstv.com
The Big Ten Conference consists of eleven Midwest universities and is the United States' oldest collegiate sports conference.

Naismith Memorial Basketball Hall of Fame
1000 West Columbus Avenue
Springfield, MA 01105
(877) 4HOOPLA (446-6752)
(413) 781-6500
Web site: http://www.hoophall.com
Named after the inventor of the game of basketball, Dr. James Naismith, the Basketball Hall of Fame is a museum that honors the most important figures and greatest players in the sport's history.

National Basketball Association (NBA)
Attn: Fan Relations
645 Fifth Avenue
New York, NY 10022
Web site: http://www.nba.com
The NBA is the world's premier professional men's basketball league. Every year, the NBA holds a draft in which the top amateur players are selected by the various professional teams.

National Collegiate Athletic Association (NCAA)
700 W. Washington Street
P.O. Box 6222
Indianapolis, IN 46206-6222
(317) 917-6222
Web site: http://www.ncaa.org
The NCAA provides oversight of collegiate athletics. It is made up of roughly 1,200 colleges and organizations, and membership is voluntary.

Web Sites

Due to the changing nature of Internet links, Rosen Publishing has developed an online list of Web sites related to the subject of this book. This site is updated regularly. Please use this link to access the list:

http://www.rosenlinks.com/imcb/bbte

FOR FURTHER READING

Albom, Mitch. *Fab Five: Basketball, Trash Talk, the American Dream.* New York, NY: Grand Central Publishing, 1994.

Carpenter, Monte. *Quotable General.* Nashville, TN: TowleHouse Publishing, 2001.

DeCock, Luke. *Great Teams in College Basketball History* (Great Teams). Chicago, IL: Raintree, 2006.

Detroit Free Press and Triumph Books. *State of Glory: Michigan State's 1999–2000 Championship Season.* Chicago, IL: Triumph Books, 2000.

Keady, Gene, and Jeff Washburn. *Gene Keady: The Truth and Nothing but the Truth.* Champaign, IL: Sports Publishing, 2005.

Kelser, Gregory, and Steve Grinczel. *Greg Kelser's Tales from Michigan State Basketball.* Champaign, IL: Sports Publishing, 2006.

NCAA. *NCAA March Madness: Cinderellas, Superstars, and Champions from the NCAA Final Four.* Chicago, IL: Triumph Books, 2004.

The News-Gazette. *Dee Brown: My Illini Years.* Champaign, IL: Sports Publishing, 2006.

Sachare, Alex. *The Basketball Hall of Fame Hoop Facts & Stats.* New York, NY: John Wiley & Sons, Inc., 1998

Stewart, Mark. *Basketball: A History of Hoops* (The Watts History of Sports). Danbury, CT: Franklin Watts, 1999.

Tate, Loren, and Jared Gelfond. *A Century of Orange and Blue: Celebrating 100 Years of Fighting Illini Basketball.* Champaign, IL: Sports Publishing, 2004.

Thomas, Keltie. *How Basketball Works.* Toronto, ON: Maple Tree Press, 2005.

Tolliver, Melanie. *Indiana University Basketball: For the Thrill of It!* Champaign, IL: Sports Publishing, 2002.

BIBLIOGRAPHY

Bentley Historical Library. "U of M Men's Basketball." 2002 (updated 2007). Retrieved May 26, 2007 (http://bentley.umich.edu/~bhl/athdept/baskmen/baskmen.htm).

Big Ten Conference. *Official Big Ten Centennial Basketball Guide.* Chicago, IL: Triumph Books, 1995.

Bjarkman, Peter C. *Big Ten Basketball.* Indianapolis, IN: Masters Press, 1995.

Connors, Timothy. "Big Bird Faces 50." University of Iowa Alumni Association. Autumn 1997. Retrieved May 28, 2007 (http://www.iowalum.com/magazine/aug04/big_bird.html).

ESPN.com. "Top 10 of the Last 10: Best Programs." 2007. Retrieved May 27, 2007 (http://sports.espn.go.com/ncb/news/story?id=2862455).

Indiana University. "2006–07 Men's Basketball Media Guide." Retrieved May 2, 2007 (http://iuhoosiers.cstv.com/sports/m-baskbl/spec-rel/0607-mbb-media-guide.html).

Michigan State University. "2006 Michigan State Men's Basketball Media Guide." Retrieved May 3, 2007 (http://msuspartans.cstv.com/sports/m-baskbl/spec-rel/06-media-guide.html).

Northwestern University. "History of NU Seal and Willie the Wildcat." 2006. Retrieved May 27, 2007 (http://www.univsvcs.northwestern.edu/trademark/history.htm).

Northwestern University. "2006–07 Prospectus." Retrieved May 3, 2007 (http://www.cstv.com/auto_pdf/p_hotos/s_chools/nw/sports/m-baskbl/auto_pdf/MBK0607Prospectus).

Ohio State University. "Brutus Turns 40." September 3, 2005. Retrieved August 13, 2007 (http://www.ohiostatebuckeyes.com/

ViewArticle.dbml?&DB_OEM_ID=17300&ATCLID=1028062&SPID=10642&SPSID=89177).

Ohio State University. "2006–07 Prospectus." Retrieved May 3, 2007 (http://www.cstv.com/auto_pdf/p_hotos/s_chools/osu/sports/m-baskbl/auto_pdf/081806#nogo).

Pennsylvania State University. "History and Year-by-Year Records. Honors and Records." Retrieved May 3, 2007 (http://gopsusports.cstv.com/sports/m-baskbl/archive/history.html).

Pennsylvania State University. "The Nittany Lion Mascot." 2006. Retrieved May 28, 2007 (http://www.psu.edu/ur/about/mascot.html).

Purdue University. "Traditions. 2006–07 Men's Basketball Media Guide." Retrieved May 2007 (http://purduesports.cstv.com).

University of Illinois. "Men's Basketball Media Guide." Retrieved May 2, 2007 (http://fightingillini.cstv.com/sports/m-baskbl/ill-m-baskbl-guide.html).

University of Iowa. "2006–07 Media Guide." Retrieved May 2, 2007 (http://hawkeyesports.cstv.com/sports/m-baskbl/iowa-m-baskbl-body.html#nogo).

University of Minnesota. "2006–07 Men's Basketball Media Guide." Retrieved May 3, 2007 (http://www.gophersports.com/ViewArticle.dbml?DB_OEM_ID=8400&KEY=&ATCLID=661063&SPID=3302&SPSID=38817).

University of Wisconsin–Madison. "Badger Notables." 2006. Retrieved May 29, 2007 (http://www.uwbadgers.com/traditions/notables_120.html#bucky).

University of Wisconsin-Madison. "2006–07 Wisconsin Men's Basketball Record Book." Retrieved May 3, 2007 (http://www.uwbadgers.com/sport_news/mbb/stats_polls/recordbook_4422.pdf).

About the Author

Gabriel Kaufman is an avid college basketball fan. Growing up in Urbana, Illinois, he followed Big Ten basketball closely and attended countless conference games at the Assembly Hall on the University of Illinois campus. He currently works in children's publishing and lives in Brooklyn, New York.

Photo Credits

Designer: Tom Forget
Photo Researcher: Marty Levick